Lighten Up
For Learning

Enjoy!

Brenda Robinson

Brenda

Order this book online at www.trafford.com
or email orders@trafford.com

Most Trafford titles are also available at major online book retailers.

Note for Librarians: A cataloguing record for this book is available from Library
and Archives Canada at www.collectionscanada.ca/amicus/index-e.html

Printed in Victoria, BC, Canada.

ISBN: 978-1-4120-9254-8 (sc)

*Our mission is to efficiently provide the world's finest, most comprehensive
book publishing service, enabling every author to experience success.
To find out how to publish your book, your way, and have it available
worldwide, visit us online at www.trafford.com*

Trafford rev. 8/14/2009

www.trafford.com

North America & international
toll-free: 1 888 232 4444 (USA & Canada)
phone: 250 383 6864 ♦ fax: 812 355 4082

Introduction

WHAT IS HAPPENING to the joy, excitement and love of learning? Why do students trudge off to school and learn only what they have to? Has school become so serious and business like that it is a chore instead of a challenge?

As a parent, grandparent and educator I am increasingly concerned that growing up, going to school, being part of a family and community is not as much fun as it could be and should be. Indeed, the emphasis in home, school and community seems to be on the old triple "E" formula. We must be efficient, effective and economical in everything we do. In order to meet this heavy criteria we have become serious, somber, responsible, dedicated and accountable. These are all strengths and positive attributes for parents, teachers and administrators.

However, today's world is filled with seriousness. People are working harder and longer. The pace, the drive and the desire for perfection are overwhelming the joy and the fun for many people. We are determined and stoical – "nose to the grindstone – shoulder to the wheel." The difficulty with that stance – that posture is that it is difficult to see what is going on around us. People don't usually smile from that position. It is becoming an intergenerational, highly contagious existence.

The triple "E" formula needs to be supplemented and complimented. We now need the 6 "E" formula. We must be efficient, effective and economical with enthusiasm, enjoyment and positive energy.

School, sports, family and community activities should not be a burden for children, teachers, parents, coaches and administrators or facilitators. For many years now, it has been my passion to explore the concepts of laughter, lightness and humour as part of the learning, growth and development of children and adults.

My five children experienced "school" in a variety of ways – not always positive. Their experiences became the basis of my exploration of "lightening up for learning." As they went to school year after year, we began to realize that the world of education is often bereft of humour and lightness. The enthusiasm and the enjoyment were missing in their day to day experiences. In fact, sometimes we missed it too.

This book has been prepared to invite other parents, grandparents, educators, coaches and administrators to think about ways to bring the joy back. Learning should be exciting, interesting, "joy filled" and just plain fun. Let this chronicle of the "school" experience challenge your thinking and your approaches to the learning environment. Lighten Up!!.

1998 Graduation Masters of Education from Simon Frasier University

1987 Robinson kids having fun on a visit to Drumheller, Alberta.

Chapter I

Lighten Up For Learning

How important is this idea that we should lighten up for learning? How did our learning environments become so serious? Where did we get the idea that learning and for that matter, growing up was a deadly serious business? We can hear how serious we are about it in some of our common sayings:

"Get serious and get some work done"
"Wipe that stupid grin off your face"
"Settle down and get serious"
"Quit fooling around and get to work"
"Stop laughing and get something done"
"Work now, play later"
"Grow up, get serious"

Sometimes I wonder if we realize the real impact of these messages. Have we lost our perspective of humour, joy, laughter and lightness in the picture we paint for young people? It's a challenge for teachers and parents to reflect on the messages we give our children.

"Someday you'll have a job like mine then you'll know what it means". (Pronounced in very sombre terms)

"Someday you'll have children too, I hope you have a child just like you". (Said in a threatening voice).

"Mommy is sorry that she has to go to work, Mommy would rather stay home with you, but poor Mommy has to go to work". (Stated with a tone of great sadness).

"If you don't get an education you'll never go anywhere or be anybody" (presented with a sense of doom).

What kind of messages are we giving them about learning, growing up and becoming adults? Sometimes I wonder why they would ever want to grow up. And why would they want to get a job? It's such a sorry sounding prospect! Or, why have children? It doesn't sound like an enjoyable thing to do.

And then, they have to go to school! It's compulsory you know. My father used to have a saying

"You can lead a horse to water, but you can't make him drink".

I've always had a similar feeling about compulsory or mandatory learning. You can always lead the learner to the learning, but can you make him/her learn? I believe as teachers, coaches, parents, counsellors, we may think we can. In fact much of our curriculum and many of our teaching plans seem to indicate that we can. Again, our sayings about learning have a very serious, sometimes threatening tone:

"It's time to settle down and get serious about learning".

"They'll have to learn or they'll pay the price".

"It's better to learn it now than pay the consequences later".

"He'll stay here until he learns".

"We'll teach him/her a thing or two, straighten him out,
smarten her up and set them on the right track".

Wow! That doesn't sound like very much fun to me. I guess I always had
it in my mind that learning and exploring went hand in hand. I also
thought that exploring and adventure were partnered activities. Then,
I foolishly expected that adventures and fun were synonymous. When
did the learning process get derailed in this logic? Many educators use
the method of "drill and test" learners are presented with one item after
another and tested to ensure that each item is learned before they can
move on to the next step. Some teachers who have become aware of the
consequences of this method refer to it as "drill and kill". It certainly
kills the sense of adventure, the joy of discovery and the celebration of
learning. This really is a serious business.

I selected the junior high classroom (grades 7, 8 & 9) as the object of a
portion of my research. I view the junior high students as the greatest
challenge. These young people range in age from 11 - 16. They are
filled with the joy of living and learning. They are at the age of great
expectations. They represent the age of innocent learning and the age
of learned innocence! They challenge, they are a challenge, and they
need to be challenged! The junior high classroom is the "space between".
They represent the duality of the learning world. They haven't yet set life
goals and their goals in life change daily. They constantly experience the
stress and strain of being "in between". They constantly receive polarized
messages "You're too young to do this and too old to do that".

The combination of emotional, physical and hormonal development
has them constantly experiencing change and diversity. The fluctuating
emotions of a junior high classroom could be compared to a hospital
emergency ward or an air traffic control room experiencing several "near
misses" each shift. In our adult world we would actively seek ways for
people to "let their hair down", "kick back and relax" or "debrief from
the stress". What happens in a junior high classroom? We tell them to
"settle down", "get to work" and ultimately "get serious".

Is getting serious the best way to deal with stress and its impact? In
extremely stressful situations, adults often relieve the stress with blue
humour, which is often "off colour". (That's one of the reasons they use

anaesthetics in surgical wards so that the patient can't hear the jokes); black humour (some of the best jokes come from undertakers); and inappropriate laughter (laughing or giggling in the wrong place or time). However, we don't give junior high students even this much space. Yet we tell them to "grow up". One teacher told me, "You have to be careful, if you ever let them get started laughing they don't know when to stop". Would that be blue, black or inappropriate or all three? So, in our attempts to prevent an occurrence of humour, fun or inappropriate laughter, we stay clear of it all! Even though we know that lightening up is the most natural way we have to deal with stress. Why should it be any different for young people than it is for adults? After all, adults are children who grew taller and wider. We all need to lighten up!

In my research I asked the researchers to spend forty hours in forty different junior high classrooms. As they sat in the classroom, they were observing the ratio between positive "lighten up" messages and negative, serious messages. My scoring method was basic and straight forward. I divided a page in half and asked them to listen intently, marking in the columns as required.

positive lighten up messages	negative, serious messages
✓ ✓	✓ ✓ ✓ ✓
✓ ✓	✓ ✓ ✓ ✓
✓ ✓	✓ ✓ ✓ ✓
✓ ✓	✓ ✓ ✓ ✓
✓ ✓	✓ ✓ ✓ ✓
✓	✓ ✓ ✓ ✓
✓	✓ ✓ ✓ ✓

The ratios were amazing and in many ways serious! In the overall study the ratio was 83 to 17. The negative messages outnumbered the positive messages 83 to 17. It must be very difficult to lighten up and celebrate the joy of learning in the face of such overwhelming negativity.

In defence of teachers, the intent was not always to be negative. In fact, in many ways it seemed like the teachers' defence. One class interaction began with these statements:

> "I don't suppose any one in here did their homework".

No answer from the class.

> "And, I don't suppose anyone who attempted their homework made any real effort".

No answer from the class.

> "Well, it's obvious that none of you caught on so we'll have to go over it again and again until you do".

Still no answer from the class…

> "Is there any chance that any one in here remembered to bring a pen or pencil to the class"?

Four or five pens were shown in reply.

> "Fine then if you didn't come here to learn, that's your problem. If you don't catch on this time you can learn in the detention room after school".

I really don't believe the teacher in question deliberately set this tone. However, we may be in the habit of creating a less than positive learning environment without even realizing it.

In schools and homes alike, we may be seriously in need of lightening up. It may be time for all of us to evaluate the seriousness of our seriousness!

1981 Sydney and Muriel Carter with grandchildren.

1986 Grandpa Syd with Jill, Leigh and cousin Brenda at
the Carter Homestead near Bethany, Manitoba.

1982 Lonnie, Leigh and Harley ready for Sunday school!

1980 Leigh taking a bath in the sink at the cabin in Minnedosa, Manitoba.

Chapter II
Getting Started Positively

A S PARENTS AND educators we often want to prepare our children for new learning experiences in just the right way. We want to protect them from disappointments, hurt feelings, failures and negative feedback. We often admonish them as they go out the door

"Be good now don't get into any trouble"

"Behave yourself"

"Be polite"

In fact, we are very concerned that they be at all times on their best behaviours, in hopes that it will prevent any misfortune. We encourage them to obey the rules, play fair, mind their own business and stay away from trouble. These are valid concerns for all of us. However, most of us learned many things through challenging the rules, enduring disappointments, surviving failures and struggling to succeed. Like the butterfly who struggles out of its cocoon, the struggle is not only worth it, but beautiful and joyful. Are we as modern parents and educators trying too hard to save our children from any struggles en route to success? Are we trying to ensure their happiness by keeping them struggle free? We find great humour and laughter as we tell and re-tell our stories of struggle and even of failure. In fact, some of our stories become even funnier in the re-telling. Still, we try hard to prevent young people from experiencing the struggle. We warn them in advance.

In this light, I reflect on Jill's first day of school. This was the long awaited day. When you are the youngest of five, it seems that everyone has gone to school without you forever. Finally, it is her turn to start, and what a glorious September day it turned out to be.

In celebration of the importance of her first day of school, I had taken the day off work. We set off to school hand in hand and I quickly found myself hard pressed to keep up as she skipped and hopped and talked non stop. She was filled with the joy of going to school - finally. Oh, she had been to playschool and kindergarten, but those were experiences for little kids. She was a big girl now, going to "real school". As I walked, she hopped backwards, precariously close to falling as she told me how much fun school was going to be. Nothing could dull her enthusiasm. I begged her to turn around. She did on the agreement that I would skip forward with her. What else could I do?

We arrived at the school yard fence. "You don't have to go any farther, Mommy", she told me with such confidence. "I can go to school all by myself from here". And off she went. I watched her little form run across the yard and into the school. I turned around to walk home, tears in my eyes - happy for her and sad for me - starting school is a big transition. This was my baby - my youngest - a turning point for both of us.

I went home to wait out the morning. I had promised to walk back and meet her at lunch time. We could come home together and have lunch. She could tell me all about school. The clock dragged - I kept busy - I went early and waited by the fence as we had agreed.

I saw her coming across the school yard - walking slowly, dragging her little feet. I waved enthusiastically and got a half smile. "Hi, Jill", I called out as she neared our meeting place. "How was your first morning at school"?

I was stunned by her reply, "I don't think I'm going back" she said in a little voice. "It doesn't sound like it's going to be very much fun". I didn't know what to say. I took her little hand and we headed home for lunch.

I decided to explore this further as we walked. "What happened at school this morning"? I asked gently. "Why do you think it won't be fun"?

Jill told me about her morning.

"Well, first we have "semblies" in the gym" she said.

"Oh - assembly" I replied. "What happened in assembly"?

"The principal told us all the things we can't do in the school", she said. "We can't run inside, we can't wear our outdoor runners inside. We can't leave our classroom without teacher. We can't go to the computer room, the library or the gym, without a grown-up. We can't bring our toys to school. We can't eat lunch - except in the lunch room".

"Oh," I replied, feeling somewhat relieved, "The principal just wants to be sure you know the rules so you will be safe and secure at school".

"Oh", she said in a non-committal voice.

"Well", I asked, "What did you do next"?

"We went to our own classrooms with our own teacher", she said, her voice still unenthusiastic.

"What happened there"? I asked, expecting a more positive note.

"Our teacher told us all the things we can't do in our classroom", she responded. She went on - "We can't chew gum or eat lunch during class. We can't talk to our friends or move around the classroom unless she says. We can't sharpen pencils unless she tells us and we can't go to the bathroom without a buddy", Jill said in that same unenthusiastic tone.

I tried again to reason with her. "Don't worry Jill", I said, "your teacher just wants to be sure you know the rules in the classroom. She wants everybody to be comfortable and considerate of each other".

"Oh", she said.

I went on hurriedly, "What happened next"? I asked, although by now I was a, little apprehensive about the answer.

Jill replied, "We went for a tour of the gym, the computer room and the library".

"Was that more fun"? I asked.

"Not really", she replied. "They told us what we can't do in the library, the computer room and the gym".

I was beginning to despair. What did you do after that'? I asked.

"We went out for recess", she told me. "We went out to the playground".

I breathed a sigh of relief. "That must have been fun". I said. "Did you make a new friend or did you play some games or go on the slide or the swings"?

"No", she said, "the playground supervisor took us on a tour of the playground so we would know where we couldn't play. I'm not allowed to play where Chris and Lonnie (older brothers) play. I'm only in Grade One and we can't go there".

My heart sank. What had happened to the joyful, skipping, chattering little girl that I had taken to school only hours before? What was I going to do with a not quite six year old Grade One dropout?

I tried half heartedly all through lunch to convince her of all the good things she would experience at school. Finally I said, "Come on with me, Jill, I'll walk with you back to school".

As we walked slowly back to the school I tried to recover her earlier enthusiasm. I said to her, "Are you going to be a big girl and walk across the yard again by yourself"?

Her answer was indicative of her attitude for the next number of years. She said, "I guess if I have to go to school I'll go but it still doesn't sound like very much fun to me".

Maybe Jill was right. Maybe school isn't very much fun. Maybe that's why we had to make school mandatory or compulsory.

What could we do to ensure that rules and policies are there to guide and direct, not to overwhelm and suppress? One teacher told me that she usually has a party on the first day of school instead of typically the last. She said she wants children to celebrate coming to school instead of celebrating leaving. She also told me it was difficult to get support from administration for this kind of planning. She told me she spends one half hour each morning encouraging children to celebrate what they learned the day before. She thinks it works much better than a formal test of learning at the end of the day. This teacher also shared with me that when a child has been away from school, they officially welcome him or her back and make a point of telling them they've been missed. She thinks it has a better effect than sending them to the office for a missed attendance report. That sounds like fun to me!

Where does it all start? It may start as early as kindergarten. Did you know that the kindergarten classroom is one of the most structured settings we experience?

Picture the kindergarten that many of our children attend. The children must line up to go into the kindergarten classroom. They must know who is ahead of them and who is behind them and they must line up in the same order every day. They "march" quietly into the classroom. The word march may seem a little severe, but they aren't allowed to hop, skip, run, push, shove or make any noise. They march quietly into the classroom.

When they enter the classroom, each child has a little cubicle with his or her name clearly marked on it. Within the little cubicle they must hang up their coat, place their outdoor shoes or boots below their coat (heels out), then place their little bag beside their boots. When they complete their cubicle, they may join circle. Joining circle is not a difficult thing to do. Their little names are clearly printed on an apple or a happy face on the floor. That is where their little butts sit. Circle is a wonderful sharing time for children. They take turns participating.

When circle time is finished, the teacher rings a little bell or claps her hands. The children then go in their designated groups of four or five to their designated play areas (water, sand, paint, blocks, or dress up) where they play for eleven minutes. At the end of their eleven minutes (it doesn't matter if their castle is half finished or they've just made a new friend), they must move on to the next play area. The curriculum calls for three different play areas per day. After play time is finished, we line them all up and wash their little hands. Then, we give them all identical snacks. After snack, they return to circle for another time of sharing.

Finally the children return to their cubicles. They reverse the process. They put their coats and boots back on. They take their little bags and line up again in the same order as before. As each child marches quietly out of the classroom, we hand them the papers to take home. They place them in their little bags and march out to their designated seats on the bus. Then, twenty years later they join our adult organizations and we say plaintively, "What's wrong with young people today - where is their initiative and creativity? Why can't they think for themselves"?

We don't always say it, but my question may be, "How did they become so structured?

Why are they so serious? Is it possible to structure the joy and light heartedness out of our learning environments? What can we do to overcome the heavy nature of our policies, procedures and systems?

I once knew a kindergarten teacher who encouraged children to throw their boots in one corner and their coats in another. She recounted the delightful scramble at the end of the day as children searched for and found their own coats and boots. She fondly pointed out the development of problem solving and decision making skills in her young 4 – 5 year old charges. However, the parents put a stop to such activities in less than a month. One parent, who was particularly annoyed, pointed out that she wanted her child to get ready for school and she didn't think he could do so by having fun finding his boots. Under pressure from the parents, the teacher returned the cubicles to the class. One mother expressed her belief that at least now her child would be protected from head lice with her <u>own</u> coat and her <u>own</u> hat in her <u>own</u> cubicle. As a mother, my experience has been that if there is head lice in the class, individual cubicles will not protect a child. Maybe Jill was right! All this structure doesn't sound like very much fun to me!

1989 Jill age 6 "I guess if I have to go to School I will, but it doesn't sound like very much fun to me".

1987 Jill's first playschool picture "She couldn't wait to go to real school!".

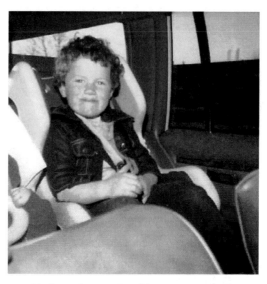

1977 Harley riding in the old station wagon "Gertie"
pretending he was the Dukes of Hazzard.

1981 Leigh, Harley and Lonnie at the Edmonton Valley Zoo.

No News is Good News

Chapter III
No News Is Good News

WHAT HAS HAPPENED to make us believe that "no news is good news"? It's true though, in many aspects of our lives. I often talk to people about their workplaces. "How are you doing on the job", I ask with sincere interest.

> "I must be doing okay", they say. "No one has called me in".

One fellow I know recently received a promotion. I was excited and happy for him.

> "How's the new job"? I asked.

> "I think I must be doing alright", he replied. "They haven't spoken to me since".

Do you remember similar experiences in school? When you were called to the principal's office did you expect good news? When my name came over the intercom, "Brenda, report to the principal's office immediately". Did I jump out of my desk and hurry to the office thinking that maybe the principal wanted to discuss next year's curriculum planning with me? Not a chance. My immediate response was fear and anxiety. What had I done wrong? Was I in trouble? Why could he/she want to talk to me? As I trudged slowly down the hallway, I carefully relived my last few days' activities.

As an adult, I've experienced the same emotions when I'm driving down the highway and the police come up behind me with flashing lights. In accordance with my conditioning, I pull over, certain of my guilt, already preparing my defence.

It happened to me one day on a wide open stretch of highway between High Prairie and Slave Lake in northern Alberta. As I passed the Faust corner, the police suddenly pulled out behind me and turned on the flashing light. I pulled over in a petulant mood. I knew I was speeding, but not by very much. I could think of better ways for the police to spend their time than chasing down perfectly good drivers on a clear, sunny day. As I stopped and searched in my glove compartment for the proper documentation, the police sped right by me on the way to something more pressing. I was thoroughly disgusted and somewhat disappointed. I had my defences up - I was ready to argue. It's a tough attitude to change. We all have it!

Sometimes we get caught up in it, even when we know better. I came home from work to discover a message on the machine. The message was from Harley's Grade 7 teacher. Please call ASAP, the message said. I waited for Harley to come home from school, I confronted him. "Harley, why do I have to call your school"? I asked. "What kind of trouble are you in"? I pushed for an answer. Perhaps I deserved the answer he gave me. He held both hands in the air, palms out as if I were arresting him. "It can't be me", he replied. "None of my teachers have spoken to me yet this term. Some of them don't even know my name yet". It is a little sad that at the tender age of 12 or 13, they have already learned the system of no news is good news. Some things haven't changed. What would Harley's reaction be if he were called to the principal's office? What if one of his teachers said, "Harley, I'd like to talk to you after class today"? How would he prepare?

In all likelihood, he would prepare in the same way I prepared for the police to approach. Maybe he would become petulant and defensive. Maybe he'd prepare an argument or a defence to suit the occasion. At any rate, it would probably not be a positive exchange to begin with. We carry these same attitudes with us later in life.

I had a boss one time who didn't understand how powerful the "no news is good news" syndrome really was. He was a non-communicator and we all felt quite safe in his silence. One day, he walked by me on his way to his office and in passing made this comment, "Brenda, come into my office at 3:00 this afternoon. There are a few things we need to go over". This was at 9:00 a.m. What do you think I did between 9:00 a.m. and 3:00 p.m.? Well, anything I did was not very productive. I checked the job ads and re-wrote my resume. However, I didn't just subscribe to "no news is good news". I was also a strong follower of "misery loves company". So, I incited the rest of the office. I went to everyone and said, "Bill wants to talk to me - he'll probably want to talk to you next. I'm supposed to go to his office at 3:00 p.m. - has he set up a time for you yet? I generated a whole environment of fear and anxiety in a few short hours. When I finally went to Bill's office at 3:00 P.M, I was defensive, apprehensive and bordering on hostile. This is the atmosphere created by "no news is good news".

In fact, my apprehension ruined my reception to what turned out to be good news. I was given a raise and a promotion. It took me several days to accept and celebrate the good news. By the way, I was reluctant to share it with anyone else. It often takes a long time to remove defensive armour - even if it wasn't needed. In addition to my negative attitude, I had created a negative setting. I now had to supervise the people I had "stirred up".

As parents and educators, what can we do to overcome this element of negativity in the learning environment? How can we lighten up the communication process and change the nature of these expectations? How can we get the learners to wear less armour and build smaller defensive walls?

One of the answers may be to emphasize the positive power of communication and interaction between students and teachers and/or students and administrators.

Perhaps we can dispel the concept of "no news is good news" by instilling the concept of "good news comes first". In many settings this means consciously ensuring good news exchanges before any bad news occurs. This may enhance prevention before intervention.

In some school systems this is labelled "catch them being good". Using this approach, some teachers and administrators actively watch for examples of good and/or positive behaviour to recognize, reward and celebrate. Participants report that in these settings, when students see a teacher or administrator approaching, they are aware that they are looking out for good behaviour. Teachers report that when they approach they observe a significant effort by students to be involved in positive/good behaviours. The naysayers of this approach maintain that as a result students "stage" good behaviours. I, for one, could think of worse things for them to stage. It has been difficult however to maintain these programs and study their longer term results.

Some teachers say they get tired of looking for good/positive behaviours. Others say they don't believe children should need to be encouraged to behave well they should do it naturally. However, in our fixation with "no news is good news", have we perhaps encouraged recognition only for negative behaviour? Have we given children a message that positive behaviour will not receive recognition? Do we perhaps enjoy seeking the negative and find it more interesting to discuss? In our policies for behaviour management there is no mention of the policy for responding to positive behaviour.

We need to break the habit. The positive things are often lighter and less serious in nature. Are we fearful of lightening up? What might happen if we try to start with the good news?

A Grade 6 teacher reported the results of her effort in the following story.

"One year in September, I decided to get a step up on the old "No news is good news syndrome". I decided to phone the parents of all of my students in the first week of school. I wanted to introduce myself and tell each parent how happy I was to be teaching their child. I got to know each of the children just a little before I called. I found at least one strength in each child with which to begin the discussion. Although six or seven of the parents I called were pleased to get the call and responded quite positively, the other 15 caught me by surprise. Here are some of the responses I received.

"Why are you calling already - he can't be in trouble yet"!

"She just started - we can't have a problem already"!

"Don't call unless you have a problem - I don't have time for this stuff".

"I thought he could get through at least the first week without a call".

"Don't you have anything better to do then call up to chat - maybe teachers are overpaid today".

"Don't call me unless there is a problem - I'll do the same for you".

"I don't know how to break this syndrome", she told me. "I don't know if I'll try this again - it is pretty disheartening, don't you think"?

That teacher did, however, persevere. She reported that she made her calls at the beginning of each term. By the fourth term, 18 of the parents greeted her call in a positive, although sometimes uncertain way. She says she will try again next year.

Should principals actually call students to the office to receive good news? What a novel idea. My daughter told me once that she had misbehaved in order to get to the principal's office. When I asked her why she chose to do that her answer was simple. "It's the only way to see inside the principal's office - I wanted to know what it was like in there".

Would it be reasonable to have each child in a school visit the principal's office for a positive reason? Would this investment change the "awe" for the position and location?

It is possible that some children are held in awe because of the number of visits they get to make? These questions challenge our thinking about "no news is good news". Is it worth the investment to minimize the petulance and defensiveness? Or - do we enjoy the power of keeping people and presumably children on edge? Why does he want to see me? Why are they calling me? Why now? Why here?

Why not!!!

1982 Harley age 6

1991 Harley's first skateboard

1982 Harley age 7

1979 Harley age3 and Leigh age 1

The Power of Positive Feedback

Chapter IV
The Power of Positive Feedback

LEIGH CAME HOME from school with her spelling test in hand. "I hate my teacher and I hate spelling" she said in that determined way of an eight year old. "Look at this stupid spelling test I got eleven wrong. I'll never learn to spell good"'. I looked at the test she held out to me. On that page she had clearly presented 100 words for the spelling test. Eleven of those words had a large red X beside them. Those words were definitely spelled wrong! As her mother, I couldn't help but be proud of the point that she had missed. She had spelled 89 words correctly. I thought she did "spell good" and I told her so. When I pointed out to her how well she had done, she at first seemed to doubt me. She said, "My teacher said I have to write out the ones I got wrong until I know how to spell them right. I hate correcting my mistakes".

It took considerable convincing to get her to think from a positive perspective. I had to show her that she had spelled 89 words correctly. I started to put red ✓ beside the 89 words. Leigh started to smile and said "I guess it won't take long for me to learn those few words will it"? On that note she started to write out those other eleven words.

What was different? Why did a stubborn eight year old change her thinking about the task at hand? What could we do to encourage this kind of thinking about errors and mistakes? The answer may be in part in learning about the power of positive feedback. But, some would say - mistakes are serious. Yes, they are, but are they corrected by serious discussion? Or, should we lighten up and take a more positive approach?

How important is positive feedback in the learning environment?

Over the years, as an educator, I have conducted the "orange peel exercise" with hundreds of people to help demonstrate this importance. To set up the exercise, I give each participant an orange, a paper napkin and a felt pen. I give the instructions as clearly and concisely as I possibly can:

> "Please peel your orange. When you have peeled your orange, please present your orange and its peelings on the paper napkin. Print your name on the paper napkin".

I repeat the instructions three times to ensure understanding.

As directed, participants peel their oranges, prepare their presentation and print their names on the napkins. It's interesting to observe that until people complete their assignment, they don't usually look around to see what others are doing. (We're well trained at school not to cheat). When they have finished, they are fascinated to realize that there are many different ways to peel an orange. As they look around the room, there are many comments made on the variety and diversity of the end result.

Then, I acquaint them with the second part of the exercise. I ask each participant to get up, move around the room and carefully observe each presentation. I ask them to choose the three presentations that they like best and be willing to explain their choice. In fact, I ask them to justify their choice with two or three reasons. Some participants express concern and even indignation at the prospect of being evaluated. I reassure them by pointing out that as we go through the learning process we are always being evaluated - even marked and scored. "Besides," I say, "This will all be positive feedback - the oranges we like best and why". They relax. It seems we all fear negative feedback.

As they wander around the room observing carefully, it is fun to listen to their exchanges. There is laughter, lightness and positive conversations as they point out things they like about the various oranges. When the evaluation is complete, they return to their places and I begin the third step in the activity.

I begin by asking a variety of participants to share their choices with the group. One participant reports:

> "I like Mike's orange because he kept the peeling all in one piece - like a slinky".

> "I also like Maureen's orange because she kept her peeling in one piece and put the peeled orange back into the peeling - like a bird in a nest".

> "I like Barb's orange because she carefully took all the white pulp off - I like a clean orange".

I thank him for his feedback and move on to another participant. He willingly shares his evaluation with the group. He reports:

> "I like Maureen's orange as well. I like the way she put the orange back in. That's neat".

> "I also like Kelly's orange because she broke it into pieces - ready to eat".

> "But I like Sam's orange best. He made a decoration out of the peelings. That takes creativity".

Once again, I thank the participant for the feedback. As I move on, asking for the next participants' feedback, a pattern begins to develop. In every group, there are certain oranges that receive more positive feedback than other oranges. And, in every group there are oranges that receive no positive feedback. I keep track of the feedback as it is provided, noting how many times each person's orange is chosen for its positive characteristics.

When I have heard from everyone, or almost everyone in the group, I move on to the next step in the exercise. This step is critical to emphasizing the importance of positive feedback. Taking with me an unpeeled orange, I approach one of the participants who received the most positive and encouraging feedback for their presentation. I hold out the orange and say:

> "Seventeen people have chosen your orange for its positive presentation. I would like to give you another orange and ask you to repeat the task of peeling and presenting the orange. Will you attempt to present it as well as last time? Are there any ways that you see that you could improve in your presentation"?

Now, keep in mind that this participant has been able to hear all of the feedback given and has had some time to reflect on it. It's fascinating to hear the results. Without hesitation, the people who receive positive feedback agree to work as hard and as well the next time. In all, but a very few situations, they also agree to seek ways to improve on their presentation the next time. Some of the comments I hear sound like this:

> "The next time I'll take more time to remove the white pulp - I could have done that".

> "I'll break mine into pieces and have it consumer ready".

> "I'll work harder to keep the peeling in one piece - I like that".

> "For my next attempt I'll do more to present the peelings in a more attractive way - I'll also remove the core and create a flower presentation".

Those participants who receive the positive, encouraging feedback are uninhibited in sharing the ways that they can improve and develop. In fact, on some occasions, people will get my attention to point out another way that they can improve, even though I've moved on to discuss it with another participant. When two participants who are sitting side by side both receive positive feedback, there will often be a side discussion between them as they reveal to each other ideas they've had for improvement. It's amazing how interested these people are in improving their presentation.

However, it is then time to approach those people who did not receive positive, encouraging feedback. Again, with an unpeeled orange in hand, I approach a participant who did not receive any feedback. Please note that the participants were not given negative or corrective feedback in any way. They just were not included in the positive feedback.

Extending the orange, I say to the participant:

> "Your orange didn't receive any positive feedback".

Quite often, at this point, I receive petulant or defensive answers such as "I know" or "I noticed" or "So what"! However, I go on immediately with the question about repeating the task. I say, "I would like to give you another orange and ask you to repeat the task of peeling and presenting the orange. What will you do to improve your presentation this time"?

Please keep in mind that although these participants received no positive feedback, they were able to hear and see all of the points made about other oranges in the room.

Again, without fail and except for a very few examples, the response is consistent and similar from all the participants. Those who received no positive feedback do one of three things. They defend their presentation; they blame their lack of feedback on the orange, the situation or me; or they devalue the task and make it unimportant with comments such as:

> "This is the way I've always peeled oranges and this is the way I'll continue to peel oranges".

> "I could have done a better job if I had a knife. It's hard to do a good job without proper equipment".

"My orange was hard to peel - it was a crappy orange to start with".

"I don't see what difference it makes. All the oranges were peeled and that was the objective. An orange is an orange is an orange".

"The next time I peel an orange I certainly won't put it on display. I don't care what other people think".

What is the difference? Why is one group so willing to improve and develop and the other group so defensive and stuck in its ways? Is positive feedback really that effective? I believe it is. What then, as parents and educators do we have to provide to establish a learning environment where young people will want to grow, improve and develop their skills?

In my research through the orange peel exercise, there have been a number of interesting side effects or spin offs. During one exercise, a fellow reached into his pocket and came out with a Swiss army knife. He proceeded to peel his orange with the finest precision. His neighbour could not help but notice. He immediately beckoned to me to come over. When I walked over he said to me, "Brenda, this guy is using a knife - that's not fair".

"I see that" I said to him. "Does it work any better than your method"?

"Of course", he replied. "You can always do a better job with a knife".

"Why don't you borrow his knife"? I asked.

"Because that would be cheating", he replied. "You should take his knife away".

It fascinated me that he would believe that because I had some authority I should prevent someone from using a tool to do a better job. Isn't it interesting the messages we carry with us as adults. Do we perhaps breed mediocre performance by our reluctance to try things that work better? Where did that start? As parents and educators we may bear some responsibility for making "fair" have many meanings.

Is it possible that our emphasis on comparisons and averages is creating a greater desire to fit into the average than to celebrate accomplishment and achievement? Is our attachment to SAT scores, class averages, international test scores, provincial standards generating more feedback about being average than feedback about strengths and abilities. If learners only compare themselves to averages, will they look at ways to improve, grow, move ahead and challenge themselves? If they are below average, they may only feel defensive and annoyed. If they are above average they may feel there is no need to strive to improve. Is feedback in averages and standards really motivating?

As parents, coaches, teachers and counsellors, we may have to look at our feedback in relation to averages and standards. Are we providing feedback that stops short of encouraging and challenging learners to move beyond mediocre performance? Is our vocabulary in learning settings too "average" directed.

In one exercise using orange peels, I experimented by providing some feedback of my own. I've regretted that experiment ever since. I was working with a group of nurses from a local hospital. I knew only one of them - Alisha. When the oranges had been handed out and the instructions given, I observed that everyone was busy peeling oranges. I approached Alisha and asked, "Are you doing your best? Are you making your best effort"? She looked at me and replied in a curt voice,

"I'm peeling the orange like you asked".

When she finished I approached her again and asked,

"Is that all you're going to do? Are you sure you're finished"?

In a less than friendly voice she asked,

"What's wrong with it – it's peeled isn't it"?

I stepped away quickly. However, I now realize the damage was done. Because I had some authority, some leadership responsibility, the rest of the group took my cue. No one chose Alisha's orange, even though it was without a doubt one of the better presentations in the room. After discussing the feedback with the group, I approached Alisha and extended to her an unpeeled orange.

"Alisha", I said, "No one picked your orange".

"Little wonder" she replied and I knew she blamed me by the tone of her voice. I couldn't blame her for that.

I tried to reach her by saying, "You're right - I shouldn't have said anything about your orange".

I offered her a second orange and asked, "Will you peel another orange, now"?

Her reply was succinct. "I doubt it"! I knew that I had a long ways to go to come back from my error. I pleaded with Alisha. "I'm sorry", I said. "I led the group to think your orange was not done to my standards. I want to make it up to you. Will you please peel another orange and give us a chance to give you unbiased feedback"?

Hesitantly she agreed. As she accepted the orange, I quickly asked the question "What will you do to improve your presentation this time"?

Her quick reply said it all. "I certainly won't show you what I've done - I don't need your help".

Wow! Did I have a learning experience that day. As parents, educators, coaches and counsellors, there is a very strong message in this for us. If we hold any position of even the slightest authority, we must be extremely careful about how, when and where we provide feedback.

Certainly, when we work with young people we have a responsibility to provide feedback, evaluate, correct, advise and assist. But, as the old saying goes - it isn't so much what we say - it's how we say it that counts.

We must continually keep in mind the power of positive feedback and the impact of negative, standardized, limited or no feedback at all. We must also be aware of who is giving the feedback and where and when and how we give it. We must also bear in mind the impact of comparison, the affect of minimum standards and the result of encouraging average as a bench mark.

1988 Chris age 7 "my 'not working' up to his potential, sometimes classroom trouble-maker, but otherwise brilliant son.

1985 Leigh age 8 "Don't worry mom I'll get there - I'm on my way"

1982 Lonnie age 3

1982 Harley age 7

Chapter V
Cheering Them on for Success

THERE IT IS again. The dreaded phone call on my answering machine. "Please call the principal at Chris' school". The tone was objective and professional - no hint of the message. Held in suspense, I waited for Chris to come home. When he arrived I queried the reason for the call.

"I can't think of anything I've done, Mom", he replied in a mystified voice. "I even passed a science test this week - not by much - but I passed. Maybe they have the wrong Chris there are three in my class sometime they get us mixed up. His voice was hopeful.

I made the call.

"Mr. Hunter? This is Chris's Mom. You asked me to call". I wanted to say something like "what the heck do you want"? But my manners are too fine tuned for that kind of behaviour.

He was so pleasant, I started to think I may have misjudged the situation. He went on in a voice filled with the confidence of an administrator and decision maker.

"My staff and I had a meeting about Chris, yesterday. And we've made a decision about Chris' learning goals and plans for the rest of the year". I was a little taken aback by the idea that they were planning for Chris without including Chris and/or his parents. Before I could say so, he added, "I tried to call you yesterday morning, but there was no one home". Of course there was no one home, I thought. We were at work. The corporate entity for parenting doesn't pay enough to support our five children. Although, I have to admit, I've always thought that parents are deserving of executive salaries. Regardless, obviously we had missed an important meeting.

"What did you decide"? I asked, trying hard to keep the defensiveness out of my voice. .

"Well", he replied, "it's about hockey". This didn't surprise me. Most of what Chris was about these days was hockey. "He loves hockey - doesn't he"? I asked hoping to establish a common point of discussion about Chris.

"That's the problem", the principal said. "His mind is so focused on hockey, he isn't paying attention in school. So we've decided you should pull him out of hockey for awhile and make him concentrate on his school work". I was reminded once again of one of my Dad's old sayings.

"You can catch more flies with honey than you can with vinegar".

Somehow I didn't think this would be an appropriate saying to bring up at this time. However, sometimes I'm not just a mother. I'm a mother bear. And in the name of protection of one of my cubs, I gave up trying to not be defensive. My reply was succinct.

"I don't believe we'll pull him out of hockey. He needs to play hockey for his own self-esteem." "When he plays hockey, he can go out on the ice for a minute or a minute and a half." "As long as he tries and does his best, when he comes back to the players' bench he'll be given two or three pats on the back and he'll be told he's a good kid." "How long", I implored, "Would he have to sit in a classroom to get that same attention"?

Mr. Hunter did not reply for what seemed like a very long time. Then he said, in a very defensive tone as well, "School is different".

What is it about school that makes it so different? Why would we in an environment of learning be reluctant to use all of the tools that we have to encourage improved performance and enhanced self-esteem? Why would we enforce a rule or restriction to try to "make" a student learn better? Maybe we should invest time in trying to understand what it would take to encourage students to want to learn.

Chris had one teacher who had a better way to capitalize on Chris' and some of his classmates' focus on hockey. He started to redesign math problems using hockey terms. For example:

> If a hockey team needs ten goals to win the points tournament, how many goals do they need to score in each of the last three games they have left to play?

> Or if a player has 56 total minutes in penalties and he/ she has played in seven games this season, what are his/ her average penalty minutes per game?

I have always been fascinated with the attention we pay to practical applicability of learning and understanding of each individual in adult education and the limited attention these concepts get in the education system for young people. Oh - we try, with a few pictures and a general smattering of childhood examples. However, we spend more time and energy trying to mould individuals to fit the general concepts than we invest trying to mould the concepts to fit individuals. Let's get their attention by bringing the classrooms and the materials alive - relating to students instead of trying to force or make the students relate to the materials.

Instead of pulling Chris out of hockey - the thing he loved most to do - I wanted to bring hockey and Chris to the classroom and use it to help him learn more effectively.

There was something else from hockey that I wanted to bring too - peer support and team work. Not only do the coaches/leaders in that environment offer pats on the back. So, too do the peers. Why is it that in most other activities that our children become involved in, their peers cheer on their efforts, celebrate their successes and generally enjoy the idea of working together. Many adults today bemoan the concept of competitive sports and other such activities. I get a sense that the negativity of competition may well be more prevalent in school than it is in extra curricular activities. I'm not promoting one or the other. I am, however, suggesting that we could learn from the strengths of both. Our learning environments have become end results oriented. We don't cheer progress nearly enough. Perhaps we leave too much responsibility for evaluation in the hands of teachers and administrators. Maybe they are forced to view evaluation too much in connection to final marks, essays and papers. I've always questioned the effectiveness of report cards. To me, they are too much like performance appraisals in the workplace.

Have you ever listened to what employees say after their performance appraisal interviews? You may hear some of these comments:

"I knew what she was going to say before she said it".

"It wouldn't matter what you do around here, you couldn't please her".

"If I was doing all those things wrong, why didn't somebody tell me before now".

"It's a waste of time - it's too late to change it now".

"I knew I was doing okay or I'd have heard about it before today".

"She never gives 5's anyhow. She doesn't believe in them. The most you'll ever get from her is a 4".

You know, it's somewhat similar to the comments you hear from students after report cards are handed out. These are some of the comments:

"She never notices the good things I do - she only records the bad stuff".

"So what if I was late five times in September. This is December and I haven't been late since".

"What does he mean I'm not working up to my potential? How does he know what my potential is"?

"Nobody ever gets an A from Mrs. Robb. She doesn't give A's".

What is our purpose with report cards and/or performance appraisals? If they are truly meant to be the basis for growth and improvement, should we evaluate again the way they are administered?

I still remember Lonnie when he brought home his first Grade 5 report card. I waited for him to tell me about it and share it with me. After school snacks were over, hockey practice came and went, music lessons were complete, dinner was cleaned up, and bed-time was imminent. Finally, I asked gently, "Lonnie, did you want to show me your report card"?

"Do I have to"? He asked with the faintest last sound of hope in his voice.

"Yes, dear", I replied and held my hand out expectantly. Out of his school bag, he pulled a crumpled piece of heavy paper with a chocolate milk stain on it. He tried to straighten the wrinkles out as he handed it to me. "You're not going to be happy", he said. "Mrs. Roma said you might kill me".

"Well", I replied with a smile and an attempt to lighten things up. "I'm glad we got your music lesson in before you die". Even that didn't bring a smile.

I opened the report card and scrutinized it carefully. Lonnie was right - it was not the stuff to make a mother glow with pride and happiness. In fact, it was awful. I tried hard to practice what I preach.

"Well, Lonnie", I said. "Let's try to figure out ways to work on this in the new semester".

Lonnie was stunned. He looked at me with doubtful eyes. "Aren't you going to yell at me first", he asked. What a negative learning environment we've created. Instead of investing his energy in setting new goals and inventing ways to improve, he was busy preparing to be yelled at or maybe even to die. A fairly serious reaction to a report card - don't you think? How can we get young people to focus on positive improvement when they feel overwhelmed with the negative consequences? This may be one of the greatest challenges for parents and educators.

This challenge always brings to mind another of my Dad's old sayings. "Don't cry over spilled milk". One of the things I've learned about children over the years is that they can't undo what has already been done. But, interestingly, they are always very interested in what's next? It never seems difficult to get a child to think about the future. They aren't nearly as interested in nostalgia as their grown up counterparts.

Could we possibly design a report card system that places more emphasis on what's next than it does on what's, past? We can certainly use marks and credits as springboards for future effort. At the same time, could we celebrate progress and success fully? Could we give A's to "A" students when they deserve it. Could we, while we're at it, encourage cheering on the sidelines. One teacher told me that the quietest time in her classroom is when she is handing out the marks. Isn't it fascinating that in so many of the other activities, the time when results are given is a time for great cheering, clapping and general celebration. Should this be a sombre, serious event or do we need to lighten up?

One of my children recounted a story about "time tests" in Grade 3. The children were asked to complete 25 math questions in a given time limit. Each time they completed a test in the time given, they moved up a level in degree of difficulty. Each day, Leigh came home and reported that a different child had moved up to a higher level.

"Robert moved to Level 3 today", she'd say. Or "Wow, Mom, Cathy moved to Level 5 today". She would describe how all the kids cheered as Cathy put a red star on the chart at the front. Knowing that Leigh struggled with math and especially with timed tests, I grew increasingly concerned as time tests went on. One day she rushed into the house, filled with excitement and shouted as she came.

"They cheered for me, today", she said. "The whole class cheered. They even gave me high fives all around". Conditioned as I was to the vocabulary of levels, I asked the question.

"What level did you get to to deserve all of that cheering"?

"Oh", she replied, "I'm not at levels yet, but I finished half of a time test. Don't worry, Mom. I'll get there - I'm on my way".

I realized at that moment, (and remembered to write it in a note to the teacher later), that Leigh's teacher was fortunate enough to recognize the importance of cheering and especially of cheering on progress. We need more teachers like her.

1987 Leigh age 10 "Most grown-ups don't believe
real stories, they like excuses better".

1981 Leigh age 4

1979 Harley (aka Count Dracula) and his little sister Leigh

1980 Leigh age 3 imitating Madonna.

Chapter VI

Celebrating Creativity

THEY WERE LATE coming home from school. Five minutes - ten minutes - half an hour. I found myself caught up in that confusion between annoyance and worry. They know the rule, I fumed - come home first and then go and play. What could be keeping them? I put their little sister in her stroller and started towards the school. There they were! I let the annoyance override the relief. "Where have you been"? I called as they came closer on their bikes.

"Leigh had a detention" the boys said in unison. "You said we all have to ride home together, so we had to wait for her". I looked at Leigh. Her eyes were brimming with tears and I knew I was going to hear all about it.

"Today was such a special day and now it's all been ruined" she blurted out. Today had been a special day. I had the day off and Leigh had come home on her bike at noon to have lunch with her little sister and I - a girls' special lunch we had called it. Their dolls had all sat at the table with us - the girl dolls that is!

I hugged her close and tried to get her to stop sobbing long enough to tell me the story. I explained to her that she would need to breathe carefully before she could talk. Before she could get her breath, her brother Lonnie relayed the whole cause of the problem.

"Leigh was late at lunch time and she had to serve a detention. You know the rules, Mom. When you're late, you get detention. She shouldn't have come home for lunch, Mom - that's why she was late". As if to ensure the seriousness of the situation, he added, "Chris and I could have been kidnapped while she was in detention, you know".

I decided to ignore the last comment. I remembered that he had not been impressed that morning when the girls' lunch was discussed. I thought I detected a note of jealousy. Besides, I knew she had left for school in plenty of time after lunch.

"What happened, dear"? I asked again, sensing she was almost ready to quit sobbing and start talking. I had to restrain myself from laughing as she relayed the tragic tale (I have to say that both Leigh and I have enjoyed this story immensely ever since).

"Well", she said, taking a deep breath. "I was riding my bike past the big pink house on my way back to school. A little white dog ran out, barking and jumping at my bike. I kicked my foot towards him to scare him away and my running shoe flew off. The little dog grabbed my shoe and started running across the lawn. I had to get my shoe, Mom, so I put my bike down on the sidewalk and chased him. I think he thought I was playing and he ran all around the yard. He was fast, Mom, and I couldn't catch him. Then, he ran into the back yard. I didn't want to go into somebody's back yard so I rang the doorbell. You know the lady who lives there, Mom, the one with the big hair. She answered the door and I had to tell her the whole story (I could just imagine). She was really nice and after I told her the story she went with me into the back yard. That stupid dog was trying to bury my runner in the garden - it was all full of dirt. The nice lady got my runner for me and cleaned it up as best she could. I put it on and went out to the front. She called for me to wait a minute and brought me a freezie. I knew I shouldn't ride with a freezie in my hand so I ate it first. We talked about dogs and how her dog didn't mean to upset me - he thought I wanted to play. I told her I forgave her dog. Then I got on my bike and started to ride to school. Then I remembered I forgot to say "Thank-You" and I know you said you should always thank people who help you or are kind to you and so I turned around and went back to her house. She had gone back inside, so I had to ring her doorbell and say "Thank You" and that's why I was late for school. And that's why I got a detention. And I don't think its fair - none of it was my fault, except maybe taking too long eating the freezie".

Her little sister and both brothers listened with rapt attention and nodded their heads in agreement. "That's right, Mom", Chris said. "She shouldn't have had a detention - she didn't do anything wrong. You should phone her teacher, Mom and tell her to take the detention back - oh - I guess it's too late to do that".

You know, I kind of had to agree with him. I decided to explore a little further. "Did you tell your teacher the story"? I asked.

"Of course I did", she said indignantly. "And, do you know what she said"? Of course we didn't know what she said, but I knew we were going to find out. She said, "Likely story you have a detention after school". Leigh started to sob again.

Lonnie was determined to get his part of the drama recognized. "Phone her, Mom - tell her that Chris and I could have been abducted while Leigh was in detention". Before I knew it, the four of them had a little chorus going, "Phone her - phone her - phone her" they chirped. As we walked home, I contemplated what to do. I decided, as is usually the case, that my children were right.

I phoned Miss Hebert and asked about the detention. She explained it in very simple terms. "Leigh was late - she gets a detention. Besides, who would believe a story like that? She probably made it up. Detentions help remind kids of the rules. They always need reminding. Besides, it's no big deal - we have 10-12 kids in detention every day for being late".

I don't think she made it up. Most 10 year olds couldn't dream up all of those details in chronological order. Besides, if she did make it up she deserves some credit for her creativity.

I wonder if it might not have had more of an impact if she had written that story down and shared it with her class. Or perhaps they could have capitalized on her returning to say "Thank You". Maybe they could have discussed the dog's behaviour. Instead, she was assigned a detention. I wanted to reward her for her creativity. I believe, over the years, we have. This has become one of those often repeated stories in our family.

I still feel a little sad, however, about her reply to my question as I tucked her into bed that night.

"What would you do differently if that same thing happened to you again"? I asked.

"I wouldn't bother to tell my teacher", she replied. "Most grownups don't believe real stories, they like excuses better".

Are we conditioning them to be defensive? Could we, as parents and teachers, accomplish more by listening to and complimenting their story telling, true or not? We need to lighten up and celebrate fantasies and creativity.

In many of our structures, systems, policies and procedures, we try to tell children what, when and even how to fantasize. When we do this we fail to recognize the true purpose of fantasy - **we try to make the real world for them, rather than letting them make their own way into the real world**. We need to encourage, build on, cheer for, validate and buy into fantasies. Fantasies are often the way children get in touch with real values, issues and feelings.

We have to get back to celebrating the ancient art of creating a story - real or not - true or not true.

A good story with the celebration of imagination goes a long way.

1984 Harley, Lonnie and Chris Halloween.

1982 Lonnie, Harley and Chris are the Battle cats!

49

1986 Lonnie age 7 "I wasn't really involved,
mom. I was just watching at first."

1993 Chris age 12 loved Hockey so much he forgot about school.

Chapter VII
Keeping a Sensible Perspective

I LOOKED AT THE clock. It was only 8:27 p.m. Lonnie's hockey game had only started at 8:00 p.m. Why was he now trudging up the driveway with his hockey bag over his shoulder? I looked out the window and saw his friend's father's van driving away. They had given him a ride to the game and I was to go later to watch the end of the game and drive them home. What had happened? Did we have the wrong time, or the wrong arena? Did the other team not show up? As soon as he came in the door, I asked, "Lonnie, what happened why are you home already"?

He gave me the story - according to Lonnie's perspective and the interesting perspective of a 15 year old male hockey player. "Oh Man", he started. "You won't believe what happened - a big brawl broke out two minutes into the game. Before we knew it, all the kids were on the ice and it was crazy, Mom. By the time they finished handing out the penalties and suspensions, there weren't enough kids left to play the game. So - they called the game and we all went home.

I was horrified a bench clearing brawl in minor hockey. I quickly asked Lonnie, "Were you involved - this brawl - you weren't fighting were you Lonnie"? I desperately wanted to believe that he wasn't - I wanted him to be the innocent bystander, just observing the actions of others.

His answer helped me and even partly reassured me. "I wasn't **really** involved, Mom", he said slowly and cautiously. "I was just watching at first. Then, Cameron started to get in trouble and I just went to rescue him, Mom. That's all I did. I just helped Cameron out - you know Cameron, Mom, sometimes he needs me to help him out.

I breathed a sigh of relief. I had somehow known that my little angel would not actively participate in a bench clearing brawl. He seemed reluctant to discuss the game any further and I wasn't sure I wanted to. I had the answer I wanted.

The next morning, Cameron came to our house to catch a ride to school. Just being friendly, I brought up last night's game fiasco.

"Cameron", I said, "Were you involved in that bench clearing brawl last night at the game"?

Without hesitation Cameron replied "I was just watching everyone else", he said. "Then I saw that Lonnie was getting into trouble, so I went to his rescue. That's all I did - I just helped Lonnie out. I didn't really get into it".

I guess they forgot to check their stories. That afternoon, I saw Murray, Cameron's dad at the shopping centre.

"Murray, were you at that game last night"? I asked. "Did you see what happened? Was it really a bench clearing brawl? Was anybody hurt? Did you see what started it"? I queried.

"There was no one hurt, fortunately", Murray replied, "mostly pushing and shoving and being mouthy with each other. But, you should have seen those two boys of ours, first two off the bench. They started it all"!

Well, I guess you had to be there. I've learned over the years that a child's perspective is just that - a child's perspective. Sometimes you can't assign right and wrong or correct and incorrect. Sometimes we just have to let some things sort themselves out Sometimes, it's better to not have all the answers. Sometimes, we just have to accept that we don't know all the answers, and we don't know who started it and we may not ever know whose fault it is.

When I was a young mother, an elderly neighbour told me the secret of coping with fights and arguments between my kids and the neighbourhood kids.

"If you leave the kids alone, they will usually work things out quickly and easily. If adults get involved, the neighbourhood feuds go on for years".

As I've watched my kids grow up and worked with young people in many, many situations, I've realized the wisdom of his statement. We need to empower our young people in more ways to be solution seekers, problem solvers and decision makers. We try to ensure no questions by giving all the answers. Every time a rule is challenged, we make another rule to prevent the challenge. Then, when they join us in the workplace, we can't understand where all the creativity and initiative have gone. What can we, as parents and educators, do to encourage and empower our children and youth to become effective problem solvers and decision makers.

Maybe Step 1 is to understand that we don't have a child's perspective - we can't see things through their eyes. Step 2 may be to accept that a child can't have an adult perspective. Their view hasn't been developed based on experiences that an adult has. Step 3 may be to understand that neither perspective is right or wrong. They just are.

We aren't talking here about hard and fast rules. We're talking about situations that require decision making. Sometimes kids are wiser than we think - we should listen to their perspective.

I was coaching in a little girl's t-ball game one day when a question arose over the interpretation of a rule. The opposing coach's perception of the rule was considerably different than that of the umpire. This discussion became charged and several other adults entered the fray. My assistant coach went over to represent our team. Several parents began to shout out their directions. The head umpire was called over from another game across the field.

In an attempt to protect these little six and seven year old girls from the sound of the battle, I called them over to gather behind the players' bench - off the diamond. I reassured them that the adults would work it out for them and then the game would go on. The minutes ticked by, the little girls became restless. Chatter turned to Barbie dolls and skipping ropes. Several bouquets of dandelions were picked. Some girls were teaching other girls how to whistle with a blade of grass. They quickly lost interest in the game completely. Realizing this, I tried to bring the conversation back to the game. With all the wisdom which comes only from a child's perspective, Amy looked over at all of the adults and said,

"Why don't all those grown-ups quit fighting and just let us kids play the game - that's what we really want to do"! A child's perspective is neither right nor wrong it just is.

Maybe we should take more opportunities to gather the child's perspective. Maybe we should ask children more often, "How would you handle this"? **or** "What do you think would work"? **or** "What would you do to make this better"? We might be pleasantly surprised at the wisdom of their answers.

As adults, we too often think that children don't know what's best or don't know what's good for them. So - we don't ask - we just tell. What would be wrong with investing in the question? If we don't like the answer, we can always go back to the adult perspective - we've got that down pat. In some schools, genuine attempts are being made to establish peer support groups and /or schoolyard peer monitors. These work well in situations where adults are willing to let the peer perspective have some impact. However, in some situations, peer supports are merely voices for adult rules and regulations. In this case, peer support is viewed as the "suck up" kids or the nerds, geeks and teachers' pets. It is difficult for adults to truly let go and celebrate application of a child's perspective. An old native saying implored people to:

> "Walk a mile in another's moccasins before passing judgment".

I think as adults we assume we can't put ourselves in our children's shoes because we know they won't fit. We should try squeezing into them sometimes. That very effort might lighten us up enough to be more innovative and creative in our problem solving and decision making.

1979 Leigh age 2

1979 Brenda with Harley and Leigh

1977 Harley " was Quick Draw McGraw"

Chapter VIII

Laughing at Ourselves

I WAS ALWAYS FASCINATED at the laughter of babies. They most often laugh at themselves - their reflection in a mirror (a baby's face must be funny - it brings smiles to everyone's face) - their own feet and hands. It is probably the only time in life when, as innocent children, we are allowed to laugh at ourselves and thoroughly enjoy it. Oh - we still like it as adults at least in other people. Red Skeleton and Bill Cosby - two of the greatest comedians made a living by getting others to laugh - mostly by laughing at themselves. They always took great pleasure in it too.

Children and young people alike need to be more in tune with the absurdity of some of the things that happen to all of us. As a parent and an educator, I'm beginning to change my assessment of the "class clown". Maybe the class "jokester" has a talent which should be shared and encouraged with others. He or she has that ability to laugh at him/herself and enjoy the laughter of others laughing with him/her.

How have we judged the class clown?

A distraction

A nuisance

A disturbance

The class clown can always find the humour, the absurdity, the silliness in a situation. If we take the time to listen to their quick one-liners or share their side stories we might find ourselves laughing, energized and filled with the joy of learning. Instead we try to squash this humorist.

One Grade 8 teacher shared with me the ways in which she encourages and yet manages the class clown. She said her most critical first step is to recognize and thank them for the role that they play. She says something like,

> "I know you are going to help us keep the light side of things in this class. I know how important that is and I want to thank you because I know there will be many times this year when you'll help me and the rest of the class keep a sensible and positive perspective".

She said she tries never to miss a chance to share the humour with the whole class. She even asks her class clown or people around him/her to share the comment or little story with the whole group. And, she said she always thanks them for doing so. This action, she confided in me, keeps a handle on side conversations and limited group laughter which can be distracting and disturbing.

She further, told me that when she is dealing with particularly difficult subject matter she often elicits help before hand from the class clowns or humorists. She encourages them to help her put some of the concepts into poems or songs or even rap to help the whole class remember them better. She says she capitalizes on the performances for results.

She maintains that as the time rolls along, she begins to see the natural humour that children have come to the fore. She says more and more children begin to see the content and learning process in a lighter way. As the young people become more comfortable, she encourages them to open each day with a "fun index" or "silly test". Children bring in quick puzzles, or riddles, or comic strips, or cartoons. She creates a laugh and learn bulletin board which is updated every week.

She told me that when she shared her ideas with her co-workers there were many doubters. An immediate question (I have to admit I worried about it too), was:

"Don't you get kids telling inappropriate or off color jokes to try to impress their classmates".

Her answer surprised me.

"Of course I do", she laughed at the memory. "We take the opportunity immediately to discuss the appropriateness of that kind of humour. Besides, it only happens once or twice and the kids get the message - they're bright kids you know. Besides", she added as an afterthought, "I get a lot of mileage out of some of those jokes in other settings".

She shared with me a really cute story about a conversation she had with the parent of a child in her class.

The parent called her and in a very angry voice started the conversation.

"What's going on in your class these days - my son told me that his friend Ben told the parrot joke in class today? I know that joke and it's not class material - what kind of class are you running anyways"?

The teacher replied in a calmer voice. "You're right, that is not an appropriate joke and when Ben told it, we discussed that it was not appropriate for the classroom. In fact, Ben apologized to the class."

"Well, I should think so", the parent went on, still wanting to make a point. "And what are you doing to make sure this kind of ridiculousness doesn't happen again"?

The teacher replied gently, "Our class had quite a discussion about humour and how it should be positive, but is sometimes negative. We especially talked about humour that is aimed at minorities or special groups. I believe it was a good learning experience".

The parent had worked up a head of steam and still went on, "I expect you to take steps to make sure this kind of stuff doesn't happen during school hours. I don't know where kids get the idea they can get away with that".

The teacher saw her chance and swooped for the kill.

"Actually", she said, "Ben told us he heard you tell that joke when he was having a sleep over with your son, Lyle, just last weekend".

The silence said it all.

This teacher believes that in fostering lightness and humour, she is fostering a more relaxed, comfortable, joyous learning environment.

What is the funniest thing that ever happened to you? As teacher's, parents and educators, we need to reflect on the responsibilities we have for being able to and wanting to laugh at ourselves. Don't let the funny or silly or ridiculous things you do or have happen to you go unshared and untold. Dig them up from your memory, write them out, fine tune them and use them in your teaching settings or at the kitchen table or when things are rough and we need a laugh. Have these stories ready - I have my yogurt story and I want to share it with you.

> I was driving home (a four hour drive) after a long, hard week. About 1/2 hour from home, I stopped for gas - and a snack. I bought a small tub of yogurt. I got back in the car and set my yogurt on the armrest between the seats of my old station wagon named "Gertie". I like the yogurt with strawberries in the bottom. The kind you have to stir up before you can eat. I stirred up my yogurt and drove out into traffic. I stopped at the next red light and took a spoonful of yogurt. I looked in the rear view mirror and thought - "that truck is coming fast - he had better slow down". I took another bite of yogurt I glanced in the rear-view mirror again and said aloud, "he'd better start slowing". I took another bite of yogurt. I looked once more and thought, "Oh no - he's going to hit me" and he did.

His truck, which had a winch on the front of it, hit my Gertie directly on the back. Gertie was pushed across the intersection into a curb at the other side. The truck followed right behind her and ended up connected to her.

The back door of the station wagon had collapsed and the winch of the truck was stuck inside the back of my station wagon. What a dilemma!

I don't know if it was the direction or the force of the hit, but the yogurt flew up in the air and landed directly on top of my head. The yogurt began to seep down my hair, my forehead and into my ears. The consistency of yogurt is such that the tub stayed on top of my head like a cap. I sat there stunned.

The driver got out of his truck and ran up to my open window. He looked at me with yogurt running down my face and announced in a horrified voice, "My God I've knocked your brains out!"

I came immediately to my own defence. "My brains are not made of strawberry yogurt" I replied. He looked at me once more and began to laugh. I glanced in the rear view mirror and couldn't help but join him. There we were - we'd just had an accident - our cars were stuck together - we were blocking traffic and we were laughing and laughing and laughing.

His wife got out of their truck. She was not amused. She said in a very harsh voice, "Henry, what the hell is going on". Neither Henry nor I could stop laughing to reply. A crowd was gathering - as everyone looked at me, they started laughing too. Even Henry's wife was laughing!

We decided to try to get the vehicles apart - Henry got in and backed his truck up - my car went with it. I put my foot on the brake, but the truck was backing up with my car attached. It all caused great gales of laughter. We decided we would have to call the police.

I don't know why it was me who had to make the call, but I went in to the Boston Pizza to call the police. When the police officer answered my call, I said to him, "There's been an accident down here at Boston Pizza. This guy hit me from behind and he's stuck in my rear end". I paused for a moment, not realizing what I had said. The police officer on the other end of the phone line was quiet as well. Then, I heard choking sounds from the other end of the phone. The choking now became a chuckle which then became a full fledged laugh. I looked across the counter at the Boston Pizza manager and clerk. They were both laughing uproariously. What else could I do - I am beyond absurd. Yogurt running out of my ears, across my glasses, and pink strawberry globs in my hair. With comments like, "stuck in my rear end", I had to laugh. I went back out to the accident site and immediately shared the story with everyone there. Most accident scenes are either quiet and subdued or angry and aggressive. My accident was different - we now had a crowd of 15 - 20 people, some leaning on cars and laughing - some sitting on curbs and laughing. Then - three police officers arrived and get out of their car laughing. They called a tow truck and obviously set the scene because the tow truck arrived with two laughing men.

How could an accident cause so much mirth? I want to give myself some of the credit. I know how to laugh at myself. I recognize absurdity in myself and in situations. I can have a humour perspective.

I'm not glad I had the accident. I'm glad I've been able to use that accident to share with my students the joy of laughing together. I find that when I finish telling this story I can ask learners to tackle tough tasks with a new perspective. I can explain that even tasks which are on the surface negative, may be from another perspective, not only be positive, but even laughable.

The stories are always worth sharing. Through these stories, we can lighten up and learn.

1977 Len and Leigh

1985 Lonnie age 6 "Miraculously, he found his glasses".

1979 Harley age 4 "I'm Harley the Grouch and I hate school!"

1977 Harley's second birthday.

Chapter IX
Tell Me the One About...

I N FAMILIES, CLASSROOMS and even in social settings, children and adults often lighten up the conversation by telling stories of strange and funny things that have happened to them.

Several teachers I talked with told me about the fun they have had with "real stories" shared between their students. It seems children love to tell stories about their families, their activities and themselves.

In an attempt to find out if my family were the only ones with these kinds of stories, I started to ask other parents and children if funny things had happened to them on the first day of school or on the way to school or even during school. I came up with dozens of examples. A friend of mine thought we should compile them under the title "A funny thing happened on the way to school". I may do that someday, but for now I wanted to share them as part of lighten up for learning.

Shelley 14 - On my first day of school in a new city I had to catch a bus, complete two transfers and walk four blocks. I studied the bus routes with my Mom before the first day. I had it down pat. I caught the first bus with no problem - I waited at the transfer point for what seemed like hours. There were lots of kids my age so I didn't worry. One girl asked me if I knew which bus to catch to St. James School. Wow! What a relief. We were going to the same school. A bus marked "special" pulled up. All the kids were getting on. "Maybe it says special because it's for school kids like us", she said to me. I agreed. We got on. The special bus took us to the zoo. The kids were a group from out of town - 3 different rural schools - they didn't know we didn't belong. We just kept going with them - we never told anyone.

I phoned my Mom from the zoo - my friend phoned her Dad. They both laughed heartily and told us to enjoy our day at the zoo. We did. My Mom picked us up at the zoo that afternoon and drove us both home. She had phoned our school for us. It was the best first day of school we ever had.

Adrian 12 - On my first day of Grade 2 in a new school I must have been really nervous. My friend Sherry and I were walking together. We found a puddle in a driveway left by a rain the night before. We took off our socks and shoes to play in the puddle. I don't know how it happened, but I walked on to school and forgot my socks and shoes. It wasn't until I got to school that I realized I was in bare feet. A nice lady in the first classroom asked me why I didn't have any shoes. I told her I had just moved to Canada from deepest, darkest Africa and we didn't wear shoes there. She found me a pair of shoes to wear for that day. I thanked her and she said that she thought I should get a pair of shoes before winter because it gets cold in Canada in the winter. I was born in Calgary, but I didn't mention that I knew about this climate.

Dennis 13 - My first day of school must have been very tiring. When I got on the bus to go home, I fell asleep. I missed my stop and rode all the way with the bus driver. Just when he got home and parked the bus, I woke up. I cried a lot and he felt sorry for me. I couldn't remember my address so we had to go back to the school and drive the whole route until I found my house. My Mom was waiting on the sidewalk. She said I looked really important - a six year old boy all alone on a 60 passenger school bus. Mom and the bus driver had a good laugh. I had to get older to see that it was funny.

Carla 10 - I could hardly wait for lunch. I knew I had a turkey sandwich, cookies and an apple. I was thirsty for my juice box too. As soon as the buzzer rang, I ran to the lunch room with my lunch bag. I opened it up to find my Dad's gym shorts and socks. All the kids laughed and shared their lunch with me. That night I told my Dad, "I hope you didn't wear my sandwich at the gym cause' I never ate your shorts and socks".

My Mom and Dad laughed really hard. They tell that story lots. I check the bags at the doorway more carefully now.

Mario 11 - When I walked home from school I could hardly wait to get my bike and meet Jason at the park. As soon as I dropped my bag off and gave my Mom a hug, I went to the back yard to get my bike. It wasn't there. I went back inside. "Mom - where's my bike", I asked. "I don't know", she answered, "I wasn't riding it". That's always my Mom's answer.

I was mad - I was sure one of my brothers had taken it. I ran three houses down to check Ryan's yard - my bike wasn't there. I checked other neighbours' yards too - my bike wasn't there. I yelled at both my brothers about "taking without asking" and they swore "on a stack of bibles" that they didn't take it. Finally, I ran to the park to meet Jason. He agreed to help me search for my bike. We never found it. When my Dad came home, he phoned the police and reported it missing.

Feeling sorry for me the next morning, my Dad drove me to school. We were early. No one else was around. And there it was - my bike - securely locked in the school bike rack. That's when I remembered - I rode it to school on the first day. Dad and I laughed for ten minutes. Dad told me not to worry - he'd call the police. I had to say I'm sorry to a few people though.

Megan 16 - I guess it's funny now, but at the time it was really embarrassing. My Dad made me hurry because he was giving me a ride to school. I was sitting in my desk in second period when I noticed I had two different shoes on one black, one brown and not even close to the same style. I went all day in socks that day. I wonder how many people noticed.

Alex 15 - I'll always remember the day I thought it was ethnic day at school. I showed up in full Ukrainian costume. Wow! Did I get everyone's attention. Ethnic day was the next day.

Sheldon 18 - One day in class I felt very tired. I put my head down and closed my eyes just for a few seconds. When I woke up, everyone was gone. The classroom was empty and the door was closed. The teacher left a big note on the chalkboard for me saying, "We didn't mean to keep you up". When I walked into class the next morning all the students and the teacher were resting their heads on their desks - snoring loudly. Then, we all started to laugh.

Maryann 17 - Our assignment was to videotape ourselves doing a 3-5 minute presentation. I worked hard on the video taping and was proud of my presentation. My topic was the negative impact of over consumption of alcohol. I introduced my topic to my class, assuring them that there would be many learning points in the video. I turned the video tape to exactly the start point I wanted. I couldn't believe my eyes - somehow my video tape had been mixed up with a video tape of my older brother's wedding stag party. Needless to say it gave a different perspective of consumption of alcoholic beverages - I had turned the video on in the middle of a "chug-a-lug" competition. What else could I do? I laughed with the group and showed my video tape the next day.

Parents, day care providers, teachers and support staff provided wonderful stories as well.

Our nanny tells a wonderful story of Harley's first day of school. She had him dressed in his new clothes ready to go. She was busy with his baby brother and asked him to wait quietly on the front step until the school bus arrived. As she finished feeding the baby, the doorbell rang. She answered the door expecting to remind Harley to be patient - the bus would soon arrive. She opened the door to greet the school bus driver - the bus had indeed arrived. Where was Harley?

The nanny and the bus driver called his name, checked the back yard, called his name more loudly, checked the neighbour's yards. Soon, other neighbours became involved in the search. Just before worry set in - the mystery was solved. Harley leaped out of the garbage can at the end of the driveway - the lid flew several feet in the air and he yelled out with great drama, "I'm Harley the Grouch and I hate school"! His clean, "new for the first day of school" clothes were dirty and rusty from crouching inside the garbage can. He definitely smelled of something not pleasant which had been in the garbage can before him. The nanny, the bus driver and the concerned neighbours broke into gales of laughter.

The nanny later told me that she wiped the major dust and grime off his face, assured the bus driver that she was "just the sitter" (glad to say that he was someone else's child), and put him on the bus. It may have been an indicator of his next few years of academic involvement. He seemed to have a trash can attitude - I think he viewed a lot of it in the same light as garbage. He left it at the curb on his way by.

However, that story has gotten a lot of mileage in our family circle.

There were some great teacher stories too. One Grade 4 teacher announced to her class in a frustrated voice, "You might as well be facing the back of the room for all the attention you are paying to me this morning". At that moment, she was called out to the hallway to speak with another teacher. When she returned to her classroom all 23 students were facing the back of the classroom. She laughed with them and carried on the lesson from a new perspective.

A Grade 9 teacher was having a particularly difficult time keeping the class attentive on a beautiful day in June. Questions went unanswered, queries were ignored. More students were looking out of the window than at the flipchart she was using. In frustration she said, "Why don't we just go outside - that's where your minds are". She said, "I guess they were listening". The room was cleared in less than a minute. She laughed and joined them outside for a new look at the lesson.

One teacher had asked the same question in three different ways and hadn't received even an attempted answer. In frustration, she said, "If we don't know the answer, we might as well go home". They did - while she was writing the answer on the board. She turned around and the room was empty. The next day they laughed and started again.

A Grade 7 Language Arts teacher confided to me that she knew her vocabulary exercise was boring. She would write a new word on the board, spell it aloud, give a definition and ask one of the students to use it in a sentence. Then she came to the word "diversification". She wrote it, spelled it and defined it. Then, she asked one of her student to use it in a sentence. He hesitated for a moment and then said, "This vocabulary exercise requires some diversification". The students watched her carefully, but as soon as she laughed, they laughed and they began to discuss different ways to learn vocabulary.

One teacher was describing teenagers in her youth for a grade 8 class. She described large, horn rimmed glasses and commented that some kids always had tape holding their glasses together. She laughed at the memory. When she came into class after lunch, all of the children who wore glasses (over half the class) had them taped on the nose piece or the arms. Someone had carefully taped the nose piece of her reading glasses on her desk. The sight of it all deserved a photograph which still hangs in her classroom.

A Mom of two boys told me a wonderful story of her problems with homework. Her son told her his teacher said he should watch TV for four hours for homework. Concerned, she phoned the teacher the next morning. What the teacher actually said was, "There are several schools being featured on the TV news tonight. Watch TV for ours". It was just a slight misinterpretation.

My favourite is the story of how Lonnie lost his glasses. Lonnie's glasses were always a challenge. They'd been stepped on, slammed in his lunch kit, left at the swings in the playground and loaned to another kid who lost his An endless stream of other misfortunes had befallen Lonnie's glasses. At the dinner table, I noticed his squinty little eyes were naked and asked for the umpteenth time, "Lonnie - where are your glasses"?

"I don't know for sure", he said. "I had them in my pocket when we were jumping over that puddle and I haven't seen them since". Holding his hand, I walked with him back to the puddle. It was deep and muddy. "Mom", he said. "I should have brought my snorkel gear". Instead, we took off our shoes and socks, waded in and used the groping method. Miraculously, he found his glasses. He cleaned them off on his t-shirt, put them on and announced, "They're just like new except for a few scratches".

I had to laugh - in fact I had learned to laugh a lot about Lonnie's glasses - otherwise, I would have cried.

It's true, we need to plan to lighten up, but sometimes if we're lucky and we let it happen - it's as spontaneous as people. Enjoy!

Chapter X

Planning for Fun in Class

WHEN I TALKED to teachers and facilitators about bringing joy and fun to their learning environments, I was awed by their creativity and inventiveness. With their permission, I will share with you a selection of their wonderful ideas.

Start with a contest

A Grade 5 teacher shared this example with me. Before her class enters in the morning she places a coloured "sticky note" on the corner of each desk (5 different colors). She uses the colors to determine the assigned work for the first class or first hour. I personally thought this sounded too simple until she let me be an observer.

> As the children came into the room, the conversations were a joy to listen to.
>
> Robert: "I've got a blue one - I had blue yesterday too - I think that's a good sign".
>
> Kevin: "I've got yellow - I've never had a yellow now for a long time - I have a good feeling about this.

Sarah: "I've got yellow, too, Kevin. Maybe us yellows will get the whole day off (everyone around her laughed).

Three children who had purple began to chant "We are the purple people - we are the purple people". Another child came from the back of the room to join the chant.

Children began randomly calling out to one another. "What do you have"? "What color are you". "There are more blues than anything else - what do you think that means"? It made me want a sticky note of my own. As the children arrived, the noise increased. Several children now had their sticky notes on their foreheads or their noses. The laughter, the chatter and the shouting continued. The purple people were now chanting at a high pitch. I felt my old conditioning take over. I approached Mrs. West who was handing out folders of assignments.

"This is pretty noisy", I said. "It must be hard to get them to settle down after this".

She challenged my old fashioned mind with two comments.

"I try to remember", she said, "that the most productive places in the world are very noisy. As for settling them down, it always seems easier if they have already had a chance to get it out of their systems. Besides", she said, "I have them in suspense".

She was right. As soon as she moved to the front, the children looked at her expectantly and as remarkable as it may seem - quietly.

"Purple people", she announced. "It's your task to find the capital city of each province and territory and mark them clearly on our big map at the back with these gold stars. Then find out four details about each capital that you can share with the class. Your presentation will be at 9:45. Please gather at the map to plan your task".

"Blue people - the felt pens await you. Please outline all of the rivers you can on this big map of Western Canada. Name them and be prepared to share four details about at least four of those rivers - pick one each. Your map and felt pens await you at the art table".

"Yellow people - choose one province that has not already been chosen. Nova Scotia and PEI are done. Make a list of 20 important facts about that province. Draw or find a picture of its flag and provincial flower, animal or bird as part of your assignment. Find your atlas and necessary materials and work at Kevin's desk".

"Where are the green people? You are tourists today. If you could visit any place you could choose in Canada, where would you visit and why? Please plan your trip - how will you get there? Map your travel for us. What will you take with you? What will you do there? Tell us why we should want to come with you. Please take 5 minutes to decide where you are going and 15 minutes to plan the trip".

"Where are my orange people? Thank you for being so patient. Melanie's mother sent us a jig saw puzzle of the Province of Quebec. I want you to start the puzzle. See how much you can get done in 20 minutes". The orange people cheered their task!

Wow! I had learned something today. These assignments would have been given anyways - the color contest just added the element of fun. I was amazed how much work was completed in 20 minutes and how willingly the information gathered was shared in the group. It worked!

I asked Mrs. West about the on-going effectiveness of the color contest. She told me she just uses variations to keep the interest up. Coloured dots under their chairs work well. Sometimes she uses decks of cards or birthstones or astrological signs. I complimented her on her creative planning. Her reply struck me as the core of my research. "Oh", she replied, "You just have to plan for the fun while you are planning the serious stuff. The process will often lighten up the content".

Thank you, Mrs. West!

Draw your question from the hat!

Entering Mr. Bright's Math classroom was a challenge for me. I had never pronounced Math and fun in the same sentence. But, I had heard stories of Mr. Bright's Grade 8 Math class and how much fun it was. I had to see this to believe it. My first reaction was that I had mistakenly entered a student lounge - the music - "Nickleback" I believe, was overwhelmingly loud. There were kids everywhere, but basically around four large tables centered by bowls of pencils, erasers, rulers, compasses and yes, even calculators. (I later asked Mr. Bright how he could keep that supply up. "Oh", he said, "This is junior high - I go through the lost and found".

The music was turned off. This was the sign. Except for some mumbling at one table, the whole group looked to Mr. Bright. He began what I thought was going to be a traditional lecture.

"Today, ladies and gentlemen, is a working day", he began. "There are twenty questions on page 73 to help us review chapter eleven. You will work with a buddy. You can determine your buddy by pulling a number out of the first hat. Each question has been written on two slips of paper in the second box. Partner up first. When you have your buddy, you and your buddy will pull five questions from the second box. Those are your questions to complete. "No Darryl, you cannot fire your buddy. For today, the two of you are attached at the math hip".

"Does everyone understand"? He asked. I supposed they did, there was already a line up at the two hats. Within five minutes the entire class was at work. I recognized the familiar banter of the age group.

"Question seven is impossible. Did anybody else get question seven"?

"It's not impossible if you have brilliant people like Mike & I working on it".

"If you're so brilliant why aren't you finished"?

"Maybe we are and we just don't want to tell you".

Mr. Bright occasionally intervened, usually with a question about progress. He prodded and assisted and applauded and supported. Each time a pair finished a question, they went back to the hat for another - always with the hope that the hard ones had been taken. One pair drew question seven and collapsed on the floor in mock despair, begging for release from question 7. Mr. Bright was unflinching although he did offer a clue. Another pair invited them to view their solution and Mr. Bright encouraged the discussion and explanation. After 20 minutes, the hat was empty and Mr. Bright reviewed the answers on the board. Most pairs had completed five questions, some only four, but Mr. Bright seemed pleased.

He then brought out two large honeydew melons. He asked each pair to draw up a plan for slicing the honeydew melons in such as way that each member of the class would get an equal piece and he and I (the guest) would get two pieces each. The plans were drawn up and presented. The melons were cut and enjoyed. The class then turned to charting some numbers on a bar chart. I chatted with Mr. Bright and complimented him. His response said it all. "Teaching and learning can be a challenge or a chore - I prefer the challenge. We generally take on challenges for the joy - I try to remember that every day. I plan for the challenge - it's more fun that way - for all of us! I suppose it would be easier, he added, to just assign five problems or questions, but this way, they did five and saw all twenty. And, they had some fun - so did I"!

Thank you, Mr. Bright.

The ABC's of our World

I joined Miss Trainor's class one day for her popular social studies activity. Each child was given a letter of the alphabet. They were asked to locate a place name that started with that letter and tell one thing about it. The activity was fast paced and enjoyable for all of us as the children called out their finds.

A is for Atlanta. They held the Olympics there once.

B is for Brazil, they grow coffee.

C is for Columbia - they grow coffee too.

Mrs. Trainor likes the general knowledge gained by the activity, but she also likes the way the children challenge each other. She says that as they do the exercise more, the children seek out more unique and remote examples.

I went by her classroom on another visit to the school and she was doing the same activity but it was now called, "The ABC's of British Columbia".

The Progressive Story

Mr. Victor showed me his version of the progressive story. His goal in his Grade 3 language arts program is to encourage creativity and ensure that each child is able to write in complete, accurate sentences.

Everyday, as part of their class, his group writes a progressive story. One child begins with an opening of two or three sentences, such as:

> "Once there were two little boys who lived beside each other. Everyday they played games together. Their best game was street hockey".

At this point, the page is passed to the next child who adds his/her two or three sentences such as:

> "My dog Chewy stole their hockey puck one day. He ran down the street with it in his mouth. They yelled at him to come back".

And so the story goes. At the end, Mr. Victor reads the story aloud to them: They laugh and laugh and laugh. Mr. Victor saves all the stories and he told me, he is often asked by the children to read certain stories over again.

I asked Mr. Victor what he does if a child says he can't think of anything to write. He said it doesn't happen often, but when it does, he just asks, "What do you think might happen next" or "What do you think of the story so far"? He then tells them to write that comment down. Some examples he gave me are:

"This story is silly and doesn't make sense".

"I don't know what to say".

He said he just reads the comments into the story - they fit and they're real. He feels that this encourages the children to express their ideas and laugh at them too!

Who Dunnit?

Mrs. Aisles, another language arts teacher shared with me the joy of her "who dunnit" writing activity. She says her grade 4 students beg to write "who dunnits".

Mrs. Aisles prepares a full sheet of paper with the 5 W's and the H on it. Each child is asked to fill in only one section or question and fold it over when completed. Therefore, the child filling in the next question doesn't know what went before. The one rule she makes is that the children must use complete sentences to write the final story.

I watched as two or three of the "who dun nit" stories took shape.

Who: Allison and Jeremy

What: bought a new car

Where: in the middle of the Pacific Ocean

When: on my birthday

Why: because they liked ice cream

How: by climbing a tree.

The final result brought shouts of laughter from the children. They loved the absurdity of it all.

> Allison and Jeremy bought a new car. They found it in the middle of the Pacific Ocean. They got it for me for my birthday and drove to my party because they liked ice cream. We saw them coming by climbing a tree.

Mrs. Aisles allowed me to keep my favourite story with its parts.

Who: the lady next door

What: yelled and screamed for hours

Where: at the video arcade

When: as the clock struck twelve

Why: because her nose got stuck

How: by chasing a cat outside.

I loved the resulting who dunnit as it was written by the children.

> The lady next door yelled and screamed for hours. She was at the video arcade and when the clock struck twelve her nose got stuck in one of the games. She is now a ghost and we see her chasing cats outside in our neighbourhood. She still noses around our arcade sometimes!

The joy of children who are having fun and learning.

Thank you Mrs. Aisles!

A Gift for a Day

Mr. Thomason takes his key questions for review each week to a local bakery. They bake his questions in fortune cookies. On Fridays, Mr. Thomason's class does their review by opening their fortune cookies and answering the questions inside. Children who are absent on Friday often ask him to save their cookies (and their questions) for Monday. He does. Review is fun in this class.

Thank you, Mr. Thomason!

You're a Poet and You Didn't Know It

Mrs. Gainsley's grade 6 classes are poetically inclined. She loves to write in rhyme and conducts her review of class materials by working with the children to write poetry about them. She gave me a poem to share:

> Verbs are action words you know
>
> Like run and paint and build and show.
>
> They usually have a subject too
>
> Like Bill, the dog, the car or "you"
>
> Some statements have an object word.
>
> "She chased the cat" - cat's the word
>
> This is the object of the verb

She pulled her bike up to the curb

A subject, verb and object blurb.

But what is curb - what does it do.

Why it's the object - of the preposition to.

She says the children collect these poems and the evidence was all around the room. She even had a laminated collection in a binder. I think I learned something that day.

Thanks, Mrs. Gainsley!

The point here is not that every day or every class has to be a "hoot". The point is we have to plan the "hoots". The good news is that it is usually as much fun for teachers as it is for learners. This lightened up environment works for all of us.Lighten Up & Communicate for Increased Learning

Chapter XI

Lighten Up & Communicate for Increased Learning

S O MANY OF our communication habits actually increase tension. This tension then gets communicated to others. We are all role models in the educational setting. What kinds of roles do our children/students see us play? Are they positive, light, constructive roles or are they serious, heavy and negative.

"I already told you that answer"

> "You'll have to correct the mistakes"

> "There's no time to explain just get started"

> "I'm not explaining it again you should know by now"

> "I'm sorry, you'll have to follow the rules"

> "You'll just have to sit there until you figure it out"

Sometimes, we need to think about a lighter script. Some of the habits we have as communicators weigh heavy on us all. Combine those habits with our tendency to see negative and express it first, and we come out pretty tired at the end of the day. I first had this conversation with a school secretary. She told me "I know exactly what you mean. I have the 'I'm sorry' habit. I generally apologize two or three times every interaction". She told me that one young student had actually called her "Miss Sorry".

"Why do you do that", I asked. "Well, I guess it's because I can't say 'yes', so I'm sorry". I feel as if I must apologize for every little thing. I worry about being impolite".

We replayed a typical call she would receive.

> Secretary: Good morning, First Avenue Public School.

> Caller: Good morning, could I speak to Mrs. Grier.

> Secretary: I'm sorry, Mrs. Greir is in class right now.

> Caller: I'm Jenny's Mom. Mrs. Greir told me to call her this morning.

> Secretary: I'm sorry, I can't disturb her when she's in class.

> Caller: Well, how am I supposed to get in touch with her? She told me to call.

> Secretary: I'm sorry. She won't be out of class until 11:50. I can give her a message then.

> Caller: So if I call at noon I can reach her?

> Secretary: I'll tell her you'll be calling at noon. I'm sorry this is so difficult.

Wow! Was she ever sorry.

I started by questioning why she felt sorry when in fact teachers are doing what they are supposed to be doing - teaching. She smiled a little and said, "I guess the parents would be pretty annoyed if the teachers sat around the lounge all day waiting for phone calls".

I agreed. However, I asked her to consider her own energy and in so doing, I asked her to reflect on her body language when she continually apologizes on the phone. Even the youngest children pick up the cues provided in body language. I pointed out to her that when we apologize, we don't straighten our shoulders, lift up our chins and smile. As a matter of fact, when we apologize we kind of sag all over. That scared her! Laughing, she asked the inevitable question. "But, if I don't apologize - what do I say"?

We re-worked that script.

> Secretary: Good morning, Fifth Avenue Public School. This is Lori-Ann.

(I suggested that because I believe when we personalize, we lighten up and sound more positive. It is difficult for us to say our own names in mean or nasty ways).

> Caller: Good morning. This is Mrs. Lowey, Jenny's Mom. Could I speak to Mrs. Grier?

> Secretary: Mrs. Grier will be out of class at 11:50. I could give her a message to call you then or would it be better for you to call back at about 12:00?

> Caller: Oh - I think it would be better for me to call her on my lunch break. She left a message for me on my answering machine last night.

> Secretary: I'll be sure to let her know you've called and I'll tell her to expect your call around

noon. Thanks, Mrs. Lowey. I'll talk to you
later.

Lori Ann was amazed. "Wow", she said, "we can do that without apologizing. I'm in"! It was a joy to work with her. She explored new scripts every day. As soon as she received information each morning, she designed a more positive way to present it.

When the principal went to a 3 day conference, her typical response would have been:

"I'm sorry. Mr. Mackey is at a conference. He won't be
back until Friday".

Now, her response is different. She says:

"Mr. Mackey will be back this Friday. Could I give him
your message then or should I put you through to Miss
Salient, our vice principal".

She confided to me that answering the phone was a lot more fun now. Besides, she says she can handle calls faster, get more done, deal with fewer difficult people **and** she doesn't think she is sagging quite as much. She has also noticed a difference in the way students approach her - she smiles more and so do they.

However, the real question came after several days of working on her new script. She said to me, "This is great. I know it's working. I just have one concern. Does this mean I have to continue to think every time I answer the phone"?

Lori Ann's dilemma is the dilemma we all face in our communications. In many ways, we have become robotic in our communication. We don't always think - we just spit it out. We get used to hearing it too.

Pay attention in any retail outlet. You find something you like. They have it in blue in size 12 and white in size 16. You would like a white in size 14. You hold the item up and approach the sales clerk. "Excuse me, do you have this in a size 14 in white"? You ask politely. Barely looking up, he/she gives you the robotic reply. "I'm sorry, all we have is out there". Does that help you? Can you take positive action at this point? No way! Instead, you put it down in the wrong place and leave the store, mumbling and muttering as you go about how they never have anything in your size. In fact, you probably tell two or three friends about your frustration.

It is interesting to note that a different script would have encouraged a totally different result. What if the salesclerk had said, instead, "I saw some white ones over here" or "I think I saw some other white ones in a size 14 at the front of the display". You would follow him/her around the store with positive interest. You might even buy something.

When will sales clerks realize that <u>we can't buy what they don't have</u>. We can't take positive action based on negative information. Neither can learners.

Maybe we should carry this same philosophy into our communication for learning. It is extremely difficult for learners to take positive action based on negative information. Or, how can learners make positive choices when the options are negative. Or, will learners take positive action if the results are going to be negative.

Think of the age old "teacher" query. "If there are no other questions, you can leave now".

Would this encourage most learners to ask a question - or two? In most classrooms, this would mean staying longer. Worse yet, it may mean the whole class would have to stay longer. What feedback would a learner get from the rest of the class? So - usually, the questions go unasked. It is difficult to take positive action in the face of negative consequences.

How about our response to a repeated question. Some teachers become annoyed by repetition and the typical response is:

"I already answered that question".

What positive action could a learner take in response to this often used statement? Somehow we've forgotten the power of repetition. The most successful communicator in the whole world is a two year old. A two year old child will ask for what he/she wants, when he/she wants it and as many times as it takes to get it. And, they usually get the results they want. I still remember a particularly determined two year old named Jill.

Jill: Mommy, can I have a cookie.

Mommy: Not now, dear, I'm getting supper.

Jill: (same tone) Mommy, can I have a cookie.

Mommy: (slightly annoyed tone) Not right now, dear, I'm getting supper.

Jill: (same tone) Mommy, can I have a cookie.

Mommy: (in frustration) Here - take a cookie and go play until supper is ready.

Who was the successful communicator? I wish I had known that script change stuff in those days. Maybe I would have tried:

"We'll have cookies for dessert after supper"

Or

"As soon as we eat supper, we'll both have a cookie".

However, most of our learners are far removed from the basic skills of a two year old. They are now grown up and serious in their communication styles. Repetition is not their model for communication. They are far more sensitive than a two year old they pick up on tone and non verbal communication. They wouldn't think of repeating a question – a second or third time in the face of our typical replies.

"Weren't you listening when I answered that before".

"If you'd listen you wouldn't have to ask twice".

"I don't have time to repeat myself over and over again".

"Didn't you get it the first time".

"Nobody else has to ask twice".

Are we really thinking of our responses when we say things like these? Or, are we just spitting out our usual replies. What kind of positive action could any learner take to any of these statements? It is, indeed, very difficult to take positive action in response to negative information. If we are lucky, they will say nothing and take no action. When we are unlucky is when children become reactive and defensive and draw negative conclusions such as:

"The teacher thinks I'm stupid".

"I shouldn't have to ask".

"The teacher doesn't want us to ask questions".

Or even worse, we may get what are commonly called the "smart alec" answers:

"If I knew the answer, I wouldn't have asked you".

"You're the teacher - you're supposed to have the answers".

"Fine - I'll never ask again".

In any case, very little positive action ever results from the negative information even when it is given out of frustration or in the face of annoyance.

Most of us as educators and/or parents would defend our actions by justifying with the lack of time we have or the number of students we have to deal with. However, as with all the other situations we discussed, we too need to be willing to make the investment to achieve the positive payback.

How much more time or energy does it take to respond with:

"Could I explain that to you again"?

"Could you work with Cindy? She will be able to help you understand".

"Could you stay for a few minutes after class and I'll make certain you understand"

"I'm glad you asked - it takes special effort to ask again".

"Thank you for asking - I'll explain it once more and everyone will be clearer".

It's an old saying, but a good one. "When one person asks a question they are usually asking for four or five others who were afraid or hesitant to ask". We should be grateful to them.

We need to understand the value of long term investment in learning. Every time we lighten up and use a positive question or a supportive response we are making that short term investment for the long term gain. Then, we can celebrate the wealth of learning.

Besides, we can't afford that negative "sag"!

We have to let go of the negative and lighten up each situation with positive words, phrases and tones.

1983 Lonnie age 4 "..for the umpteenth time, Lonnie where are your glasses?"

1978 Harley and Leigh

1985Len and a "particularly determined two year old named Jill"

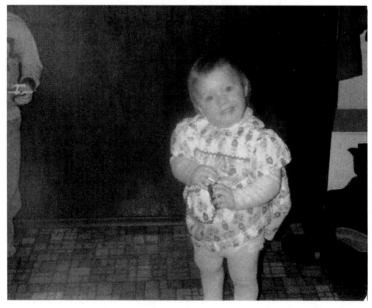

1984 Jill 1 year old

Chapter XII
Parent Teacher Interviews

S PEAKING OF LIGHTENING up the learning environment, I've learned a little technique to lighten up and create a more positive setting for the parent teacher interview. It's a good technique for parents. I think it could be reversed for teachers too!

As parent teacher interview time approaches, plan for a positive interaction. This has not always been easy in our family because although our children are wonderful to us, they have not always been academically awe inspiring or wonderful in terms of school behaviour standards. The parent-teacher interview has most often been used to discuss these lapses or short comings. I had learned to dread them, often ending up feeling defensive and less than worthy as a parent. Quite often I had to admit that I didn't know what they were talking about (I had probably heard the story from a child's perspective). I also was unaware of several of the issues at hand (my children had perhaps forgotten to tell me the whole story). Furthermore, I was forced to admit that I didn't know what to do about it. (Most of the sins had already been committed and I felt immensely incapable of changing the past). Worse than that, I felt frustrated at not being able to talk about the future except for being asked to make promises that I was uncertain I could make my children live up to. Most of all, I felt protective, annoyed and not listened to. Why couldn't other people realize just how wonderful these children are?

Then another Mom shared her secret with me. It seems her children's academic achievement was not always awe inspiring either. Now I plan differently.

Before I go to the parent teacher interview, I sit down with the child in question and ask for information to take with me. A most recent situation involved Chris, my "not working" up to his potential, sometimes classroom trouble maker, but otherwise brilliant son.

"Chris, I need to ask you an important question". I start out to get his attention. "Tell me, before I go to the parent-teacher interview, what do you like best about Miss French"?

Chris stares at me and I want to check the mirror for foreign objects on my face. "Go ahead", I said, "Tell me what you like best about Miss French"?

"Are you kidding me, Mom"? He whines in a voice of incredulous doubt. "There is nothing to like about Miss French. Wait until you meet her - you won't like her either".

Not to be deterred I push a little bit by saying, "Chris I'm not asking for a dozen references - I just want to know what you like about Miss French - there must be something positive".

"Mom", he says patiently. "You must be conducting some kind of research and I don't want to be a part of it. Miss French gave me 32 in Science. She has phoned here three times already to say I'm being inappropriate in class. There is nothing I can tell you".

This is going to be harder than I had anticipated. But, I'm determined to try my new technique.

"Please, Chris", I plead, "Think really hard - there must be something positive you can tell me. You've been in her class for three months".

Almost in exasperation he says slowly, "Well, when you forget your pen or your calculator, Miss French has extras she'll lend out for the class. I forget stuff a lot, so I like that about her".

"That's great, Chris", I tell him. "That's all I need - I'll let you know what happens".

That evening I set off for the school gym and the parent teacher interview with a lighter heart and a more positive outlook.

I lined up to see Miss French. Judging by the length of the line and the expression on the faces of the parents and Miss French, I decided that Chris was not the only difficult student she had. It's amazing how quickly we fall into "Misery loves company".

Finally, it was my turn. I slipped into the parent chair and extended my hand.

"I'm Chris' Mom", I said.

Miss French nodded her head and extended to me a sincere look of sympathy - or was it empathy. Then, I began to follow through on my plan. I said to Miss French, "Before I came here tonight I sat down and talked to Chris. I asked him what he likes best about you and about being in your class. Do you know what he said"?

I'm not certain, but I think her mouth dropped open and I heard an audible gasp for breath. She was not expecting this approach. She didn't reply.

I went on and said to her, "Chris told me that what he likes best about you is that when he forgets a pen or his calculator, you will lend him one for class. He appreciates that and I want you to know that his Dad and I appreciate that too. Now, before we go on, will you tell me, what is that you like best about Chris"?

After a long pause and some reflection, she finally said, "Chris has a great sense of humour and he writes clearly and naturally". I agreed with her and for the next fifteen minutes we talked mostly about Chris' writing skills - his creativity, his vocabulary and his delightful sense of humour.

Towards the end of my fifteen minute time slot we agreed that Chris needed to spend some dedicated time catching up on Chapters 12 - 15 in his Science text. I also agreed to post the list of assigned deadlines she gave me on the fridge and help remind Chris to get his assignments in on time. I found out that he was doing the assignments well - he just kept forgetting to hand them in.

That evening when I went home, I told Chris all about our conversation. I told him about the good things Miss French said about his writing skills, his creativity and his sense of humour. We talked about deadlines. A few weeks later, Chris told me that he showed Miss French a science fiction story he had written. He said she read it to the class. I didn't hear from Miss French that term, but Chris' mark went up to 58. At the next interview, she told me that Chris got nearly all of his assignments in on time.

What a difference a positive approach can make. My children are now used to it. When the date nears for parent teacher interviews, they often say:

"We know, Mom, you want to know what I like about Mr. Mackey. It wasn't easy, but I have thought of a few things for you. Let me know what he says - I could be doing better in his class".

All of us in our liaison with our children's learning environment could benefit from a more positive approach. Plan for a positive exchange and you may be pleased at the positive results. Lighten up your approach and look forward to the parent teacher interview.

1983 Jill playing on the beach in Minnedosa, Manitoba.

1987 Jill "Mommy, could I have a cookie?

1989 Jill age 6 with her imagination and a marker.

1985 Leigh age 8

1981 Harley age 6 very serious baseball player and future serious golfer.

1987 Harley, Lonnie, Leigh, Chris and Jill Christmas

Prologue

A SPECIAL THANK YOU to all of the teachers, administrators, parents and students who shared their stories and experiences. Although their names have been changed, their stories remain an important part of this research.

A special thank you to my children Harley, Leigh, Lonnie, Chris and Jill for allowing me to use their names and their stories. They are REAL.

Lighten Up for Learning!!

1989 Classic family picture

1979Leigh age 2 and Harley age 4 wearing
Grandma's homemade superman outfits

1989 Lonnie showing off his first remote controlled car.

1980 Leigh, Lonnie and Harley "Rub a dub dub!"

1979 Grandpa Syd holding Lonnie age 4 months.